T0277082

Check
That Fact

SUPER
QUICK
SKILLS

Check That Fact

Sarah
Morris

Los Angeles | London | New Delhi
Singapore | Washington DC | Melbourne

Los Angeles | London | New Delhi
Singapore | Washington DC | Melbourne

SAGE Publications Ltd
1 Oliver's Yard
55 City Road
London EC1Y 1SP

SAGE Publications Inc.
2455 Teller Road
Thousand Oaks, California 91320

SAGE Publications India Pvt Ltd
B 1/I 1 Mohan Cooperative Industrial Area
Mathura Road
New Delhi 110 044

SAGE Publications Asia-Pacific Pte Ltd
3 Church Street
#10-04 Samsung Hub
Singapore 049483

Editor: Jai Seaman
Senior assistant editor: Charlotte Bush
Production editor: Victoria Nicholas
Marketing manager: Catherine Slinn
Cover design: Shaun Mercier
Typeset by: C&M Digitals (P) Ltd, Chennai, India

Library of Congress Control Number: 2021931883

British Library Cataloguing in Publication data

A catalogue record for this book is available from
the British Library

ISBN 978-1-5297-5978-5 (pbk)

Contents

Everything in
this book!

Ensuring that you can find, identify, and use appropriate and credible
sources is an important part of conducting research.

You don't want to use faulty evidence or share bogus information with
others. Being able to critically evaluate sources and identify credible
information is a key part of being a savvy researcher.

There's a lot of questionable and inaccurate information floating around
online. Use critical evaluation skills to make sure that you can tell the
difference between credible and non-credible information.

Sources are created in different ways and have different features.
Learning to identify these differences can help you select and evaluate
sources for your own research project.

Section 5   How can I learn more about who created my source?

Learn techniques to help you identify and evaluate the credentials of who created your source.

Section 6   How can I fact-check a claim?

Don't just take claims at face value. An important part of evaluating sources is knowing how to fact-check claims and ensure that your source is credible.

Section 7   How can I identify the purpose of a source?

Just as there are a wide range of source types, there are a wide variety of purposes behind a source. Use different techniques to identify and better understand the purpose of a source so that you can fully understand what you are using for your own research project.

Section 8   How do I know if a source is worth using?

Sources come in a lot of different forms and not all sources are going to be appropriate for your research needs. You can use different techniques to ensure that you select the best sources for your research.

Why do I need to use sources?

10 second
summary

Sources are an essential part of research. Sources can help you learn more about an issue, back up a claim, and share your ideas with others.

60 second summary

Sources are the foundation of your research project. You can use your sources to provide evidence and support for your claims and ideas, and your sources can help you articulate and share your ideas with others.

There are two key things to remember about research: research is a problem-solving process and research is a conversation. We conduct research to explore ideas, discover new things, and to share ideas and potential solutions to issues. Whether you're trying to consider the impact of an historical event, propose a new way to treat an illness, or analyse the results of an experiment, research is a way to explore and share solutions, insights, and ideas. With research, you can share your ideas, but you also respond to other people's ideas in your work.

Sources as evidence and as … conversation starters?

We conduct research to learn new things, to solve problems, and to engage in conversations. When you're proposing a new idea, sharing some analysis, or suggesting a solution to something, you want people to take your ideas seriously and to listen to what you have to say. And sources can help with this! Sources can act as evidence to support your claims and ideas. This is why ensuring that your sources are accurate, credible, and appropriate for your research project is so important.

Source Material that you can use to provide evidence in a research project or to fulfil an information need. Sources can come in many forms and can be used for a variety of purposes.

But sources also play another vital role in another aspect of research. When you're researching, you end up responding to other sources. You might agree with their thesis, or criticize some aspect of their analysis, or debate their take on an issue. And other people can respond to your research as well. The sources you use for your research project are part of the different conversations happening around your research topic.

You might end up responding to different sources in a wide variety of ways in your own research project. You might agree, disagree, debate, critique, celebrate, question, or challenge a given source. Think of it as a boisterous dinner where you're discussing a topic and everyone has a strong opinion and a lot to say. As a researcher, you are sifting through these conversations and ideas, responding with your own thoughts, and then sharing all of those ideas and thoughts with your audience.

Opinion A belief or a view that may or may not be based on fact.

You don't select sources in a vacuum

Every research project will have unique needs. You'll consider the following for each research project (think of it as a bit of a recipe):

1. A topic
2. Research questions
3. Main points you're trying to make
4. Parameters, like how long you have to work on this project
5. How you'll be sharing your ideas (A paper? A poster? A website?)
6. Who the audience is for your research (Your professor? Attendees at a conference?)
7. The information you need for your research project

You'll need different types of sources for your different research needs and thinking about this as you get started can help you make sure that you are finding exactly what you need to ensure your research is successful. Maybe you need sources to help you answer a question, maybe you're exploring a challenging issue and want to understand the debates around a topic, or maybe you need statistics to help you illustrate a point. Thinking through your information needs can help you find the best sources for your project.

You can use sources for a lot of different things

Sources are a key part of research projects. But, research projects, just like sources, can come in lots of different forms! You might need to find and use sources for a research paper, but you might also need to find a source to help you support a claim you are making on social media or to help you make a decision about a personal issue. Being able to figure out what you need and making sure that information is accurate and credible is a vitally important part of being a strong researcher, whether your research project is big or small.

Don't get overwhelmed – have a plan

Sources are definitely an important part of research projects. But trying to find the sources you need can be really challenging. It can sometimes feel like trying to find a needle in a haystack. Other times, it can feel like turning on a firehose. Taking some time to reflect on your research project and your research needs and questions can help you feel less overwhelmed and give you a better sense of what you're trying to look for.

A student told us

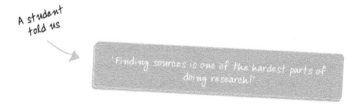

'Finding sources is one of the hardest parts of doing research!'

Try to think about what you need and what your project is about so you don't feel as overwhelmed. It's easier to search for sources if you have some goals in mind.

'Take the time to make a plan at the start of a project so you can avoid feeling overwhelmed later!'

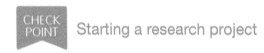

There are a lot of questions to consider when you are starting a research project. Use this checklist to help you keep track of questions you might need to consider for your particular research project. Tick the ones you've done.

☐ What is my research topic?

☐ What are my research questions?

☐ What are the goals of my research project? What am I trying to accomplish?

☐ What are some of the main points I want to highlight in my research?

☐ Who is the audience for my research project?

☐ How will I communicate my research?

☐ What types of information do I need to help me with my project?

☐ Where can I go to find the information I need?

ACTIVITY Source needs assessment

Answer the following questions when you are embarking on a research project to help you ensure that you are finding and using credible sources.

What is your research topic?

Research topic:

....

....

....

What are your research questions?

Research question(s):

....

....

....

What are your goals for your research?

Research goals:

....

....

....

Consider the types of sources you might need to find for your research project to be successful and then think of a plan for finding those sources. Where will you go to look for your different types of sources? Add your ideas in the table below.

Hint: see Section 4 if you need inspiration for the types of sources you might need.

Source type	Search strategy: where can you find this type of source?

Why do I need to evaluate sources?

10 second summary

You want to make sure that you are using credible, accurate, and appropriate information in your research so that others take your ideas and claims seriously.

It's not enough to just find any old source; you want to make sure you're finding the best sources for your project. There is a lot of information and sources in the world. And the information and sources that exist can vary wildly in terms of quality. When you are researching a topic, you can come across everything from award-winning publications to conspiracy theories. And when you are conducting research, whether you are writing a paper for a class, trying to put together a report for your boss, posting about an issue on social media, or just trying to solve a personal problem, you want to make sure that you are finding and using credible information that is right for your project.

Good sources vs. bad sources

Research would be much, much easier if there were good sources and bad sources. You could just clearly label every source accordingly and then just go find the good ones for your paper. Ta-da! Unfortunately, the reality is more complicated. Sources can

Evaluate To assess or analyse something. In the context of evaluating sources, evaluation means determining whether or not a source is credible.

be distinguished by a variety of factors and features and, as a researcher, you need to evaluate sources with a variety of different questions in mind.

1. First, it is important to evaluate sources for credibility

This is probably what most people think of when it comes to evaluating sources, and it gets close to the good vs. bad distinction. Credibility adds more nuance to the discussion though. A credible source is one that is accurate, trustworthy, and factual. When you are evaluating a source for credibility, you are trying to determine whether or not the source is accurate and trustworthy.

Credibility Something that is trusted and believed in. Credible sources have factors, such as accuracy and expertise, that help people view them as trustworthy.

Factual Something that is true and focuses on reality and what is actually the case, rather than interpretation.

- Are the claims valid?

- Is the information true?

- Is the argument well-reasoned?

- Does the source feature expertise?

Meanwhile, a non-credible source is one that is inaccurate, untrustworthy, and not factual. A non-credible source might make bogus or outlandish claims, spread falsehoods, feature a lack of expertise or knowledge on a topic, or make a poorly reasoned argument.

Is the source the best fit for your research projects and your information need? Does the source help you prove a point, bolster a claim, or serve some sort of purpose in your research project? Depending on your research project, you might need different types of sources, including non-credible sources. For instance, you might be using a non-credible source as an example of something or to help you argue a point.

The important thing is that you understand the source, what it is, what it is saying, and whether or not it is credible, and that you are accurately representing the source to your audience. You don't want to take a non-credible source and try to pass it off as credible or trustworthy in your own research project.

Your role as a researcher

It is vital to take the time to evaluate your sources to ensure that you are using the best sources for your project. You want to make sure that you are using credible information and that you are selecting sources that are right for your project. Being able to select and use appropriate sources is a key part of being a successful and strong researcher. Here are some reasons why your source evaluation skills matter:

- **Academic reputation** – You don't want to hand in assignments and research papers that feature non-credible sources. Citing a conspiracy theory is not going to earn you top marks in a class.

Conspiracy theory A belief in some sort of idea or explanation that is false and is not based in fact or reality.

- **Professional reputation** – In the future, you want to have a reputation as someone who is a strong researcher. You don't want to submit a report or share something in a public arena that is inaccurate or just completely wrong.

- **Your role as a digital citizen** – All of us are consumers and producers of information online, particularly if you are a user of any sort of social media. Misinformation, conspiracy theories, rumours, and other forms of false information are a growing problem in online spaces. As people who participate in online spaces, as digital citizens, we can all work to ensure that we are sharing accurate information with others online.

Digital citizen

Someone using digital tools and information technology to engage in society and in different social and political issues.

Misinformation

False or inaccurate information that may deliberately try to deceive someone.

Source evaluation and information literacy skills

Source evaluation is one aspect of something known as information literacy skills. Information literacy is the ability to find, evaluate, use, and create information, and it is a central skill set for researchers to possess. Information literacy skills can also help empower you as a digital citizen and help you become better at navigating the sea of information online. Finding, evaluating, and using information isn't always easy. There are a lot of questions

Information literacy

A skill set that involves the ability to find, use, evaluate, produce, and share information in a variety of formats.

to consider and things to keep in mind, and sometimes it can be hard to determine what a source is or how credible a source is. But, with practice you can get faster and savvier at evaluating sources, and you can become a more confident researcher.

'Evaluating sources can feel complicated and time-consuming, but it really pays off when you have a rock-solid selection of sources for your assignment.'

This is very true! And you will get faster at evaluating sources with practice.

'Always be willing to delve a little deeper and not just take things at face-value.'

CHECK
POINT — Evaluating sources

Test your knowledge and answer the following questions:

• Why is it important to evaluate sources for research projects?

....

....

....

....

....

....

• Why is it important to evaluate sources you find online, even if you
  aren't using the source for something like a research paper?

....

....

....

....

....

....

Answers

Answer 1 – Evaluating sources can help you ensure that you are using credible information and that the source you've selected is the right kind of source for your research project.

Answer 2 – There is a wide variety of information online, and some sources are more accurate and credible than other sources. By taking time to evaluate sources, you can make sure that you are consuming accurate information and that you are sharing accurate information with others!

Congratulations!

You now know why sources matter, how you can use sources in your research projects, and why it is important to evaluate sources. Armed with this knowledge, you can now start honing your evaluation skills and learn to identify the best sources for your research projects.

How do I know if a source is credible?

10 second
summary

You can use a series of questions and
criteria to examine the who, what, when,
why, and how of a source and determine
whether or not a source is credible.

Being able to distinguish between credible and non-credible sources is one of the most important skills you can have. It's a bold statement but a true one. There's a lot of non-credible information out there and the challenges around misinformation are growing. It's vitally important to be able to identify credible information and communicate that information out to others.

Credible sources are not a one size fits all situation (though it would be nice if they were!). But credible sources tend to have certain factors or features that you can learn to recognize, just as you can learn to recognize certain warning signs around non-credible sources. In a nutshell, credible sources are produced by people who have expertise or knowledge on the topic, and they share fact-based and truthful information.

Credibility indicators

Credible sources are sources that are produced by experts and individuals with knowledge of a topic and are factual and truthful. You can of course have credible sources that are opinion pieces, for instance, but that credible opinion piece would still be sharing information rooted in facts, as opposed to a source sharing an opinion that is based on a conspiracy theory. In contrast to credible sources, non-credible sources tend to raise questions and red flags. Maybe there is no author at all or the author has questionable credentials. Maybe there are no citations or references to be found to provide evidence to a claim. So how can you tell what is credible and what isn't? There are a few guiding questions that you can ask yourself.

Key criteria for identifying credible sources

There are a lot of lists out there to help you evaluate a source. Here is a list that uses some easy-to-remember questions to help you evaluate a source and decide if it is credible:

- Who produced this source? What is their reputation and expertise?

- What type of source is this? What are you looking at?

- When was this source produced? Is the information still relevant?

- Why was this source produced? What is the purpose and goal of the source?

- Where did you find this source? Did it come from a reputable or trusted location?

Let's see a few examples of these criteria in action:

- **Who:** are you reading an article on a medical topic that was written by someone with a PhD (a good sign!) or someone known to promote unscientific and dangerous health remedies (not so good!)?

- **What:** is your source an article from a reputable newspaper or is the source a rant from an unknown person on social media?

- **When:** was your article on psychiatric treatments written in 2010 or in 1910?

- **Why:** was your source written to provide information or was your source written to try to sneakily sell you something?

- **Where:** did you find your source using a database at your library or did you randomly come across it on social media?

Identifying credible sources – self-reflection

When evaluating sources, it is also very important to reflect on your own knowledge, expertise, beliefs, and biases. You might be

> Bias Strong weight in favour of, or against, a certain idea or topic.

more or less likely to get fooled by a non-credible source if you aren't familiar with the topic, or if a topic is really emotional for you and you are therefore less able to critically analyse a source. Here are a few questions you can ask yourself when you are confronted by a source:

- **What do I know about this topic?** If you have expertise in the topic, you might be able to quickly discern if the information is credible. However, if the topic is unfamiliar to you, you might want to double check the claims or make sure you understand what you are reading before you make a decision.

- **What am I feeling or experiencing right now?** If you are having a very strong emotional reaction, you might want to pause for a beat and reflect on why that is. Misinformation, for instance, can be very emotionally manipulative. You want to be able to clearly evaluate a source and not get caught up in loving what the source says and not bothering to check on the source's accuracy, for example. Being aware of your own knowledge, emotions, and reactions to sources you encounter can help you avoid getting fooled by non-credible information.

Complicating factors

Remember, credible and non-credible sources can take different forms. A key part of evaluating sources effectively is to critically analyse and understand what you are seeing. Let's see some examples of different types of credible sources:

- A credible scientific study – part of the credibility of this source hinges on how well the study was performed. Was the research method sound? Are the results presented accurately?

- A credible social media post, where someone is sharing their thoughts on an article – part of the credibility of this example hinges on the article that the person chose to share on social media and whether or not that article is sharing factual information. But the credibility of this post is also impacted by the poster's comments on the article, and whether or not those are well-reasoned.

As you can see, credible sources can come in lots of different forms and involve different factors of credibility. Non-credible sources can also come in lots of different forms, from conspiracy theories that are completely inaccurate and harmful, to an article with a misleading headline which can cause confusion, to a study that offers a poor interpretation of data.

A student told us

'Keeping in mind a few basic questions and things to look for gives you a starting place and can make evaluating a source a lot easier!'

Absolutely! Asking a few basic questions when you are evaluating something, such as who wrote it, can give you a lot of insight into a source. Remember, evaluating sources doesn't need to be overly complex.

'If you know the questions to ask, you can find what you need.'

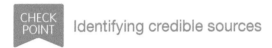
CHECK POINT — Identifying credible sources

Think about what you are studying. In your field or area of study, what are some of the things you pay attention to in order to determine whether or not an article is credible? Make a list below:

....

....

....

....

....

....

....

....

....

....

....

....

....

....

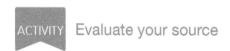

ACTIVITY Evaluate your source

Evaluate your source by answering these questions!

First, provide some basic information on your source:

Title: ....

Author: ....

Now, do some self-reflection:

- What do you know about this topic? Do you know a lot or only a little?

....

....

- Is the source familiar to you?

....

....

- What are your first impressions of this source? What are you noticing?

....

....

- Pause: based on your self-reflection, do you need to do a more in-depth fact-check? If yes, spend more time with the questions on the next page!

Finally, answer these credibility indicator questions:

- Who wrote or published this source? What is their reputation?

....

....

- What type of source is this?

....

....

- When was the source published? Is it current and relevant?

....

....

- Why was this source produced? What are the goals?

....

....

- Where did you find this source?

....

....

- Based on everything you've noted, what is your overall verdict? Is this source credible?

....

....

How can I tell what type of source I am looking at?

10 second summary

Sources come in many different types, and each type of source boasts unique facets. Recognizing different types of sources can help you better select sources for your research.

60 second
summary

The different types of sources all feature distinguishing features and unique aspects that are worth recognizing. Being able to identify and recognize different types of sources is a key aspect of being able to evaluate sources effectively. If you don't know what you are looking at, or how it was produced, you might have a hard time knowing what credibility indicators, or red flags, to look out for in your evaluation. Some sources, such as scholarly sources, go through rigorous review processes to ensure they are accurate. Other types of sources might have no review process at all. Recognizing what something is or isn't can help you make a solid judgment on a source's credibility without looking for things that aren't there, making assumptions, or misunderstanding the nature of a source.

A type of source that you are likely to have encountered as a student is a scholarly source. Scholarly sources are also called academic sources or peer-reviewed sources. In a nutshell, a scholarly source is something that is produced by an expert in a given subject area and that goes through peer review, a process where other experts review the source and make sure it is accurate and credible. How can you identify a scholarly source?

Scholarly source An academic source that is written by experts and is subject to peer review.

Peer review A review process where experts in a field review the work of another expert to ensure that it is accurate and worthy of publication.

- **The author** – often the author or authors will have a PhD or credentials in a field.

- **The publication** – scholarly sources are typically found in scholarly journals.

- **The peer review process** – academic journals will often indicate they are peer-reviewed, and many databases will label academic journals or scholarly articles as peer-reviewed.

Generally speaking, scholarly sources are credible sources and ones that go through a rigorous review process. However, it is still good to check on the reputation of the author or authors, see when it was published (is the information current and relevant?), and examine other credibility indicators to be sure your particular scholarly source is credible and relevant to your research needs.

On the other hand, popular sources get much more complicated. A popular source is essentially not a scholarly source. Which sounds easy enough. But this means that a popular source can be a lot of different

Popular source A wide range of sources that are not scholarly. Popular sources vary greatly in terms of type and credibility.

things! Popular sources include: award-winning newspapers, tabloids and gossip magazines; social media; infographics; videos; and pretty much any type of media content you might encounter. Some popular sources go through editorial review, for instance, articles in news magazines are reviewed by an editor. But other popular sources might go through no review at all and the person creating the source might have no credentials or background in the topic. Since popular sources can range dramatically in terms of what they are and how credible they are, it is good to take some extra time when you are evaluating a popular source to be sure you understand what the source is and whether or not it is credible.

Other types of sources

Here are some other types of sources that you might encounter and use in a research project:

- **Trade publication** – These are sources where the target audience is someone who works in a particular trade industry, such as manufacturing or publishing. A trade publication will keep people in that industry up to date with news and developments.

Trade publication
A publication that focuses on providing news, updates, and information for a specific industry.

- **Reviews** – A source where someone is commenting on and critiquing another source. Reviews come in lots of different forms. You might have a film review written by a film critic or a scholar providing a review of another scholar's book.

- **Primary source** – A primary source is produced at a particular time and might provide a contemporaneous account of an event. For instance, diaries, old newspaper articles, a newsreel, or an audio recording could be primary sources.

> **Primary source**
> A source of information created at a time of study. Primary sources can take many forms, such as diaries, letters, or newsreel footage, and may provide a first-hand account of a past event or a topic.

- **Encyclopedias** – Encyclopedias are reference works, and they are designed to provide a factual overview of a topic. You can use encyclopedias to get information on a topic and they don't provide arguments or commentary.

Complicated sources

Some sources are more complicated than others! One example of a particularly tricky type of source is sponsored content. Sponsored content is where a source is sponsored by a company or industry. It can sometimes be tricky to tell if something is sponsored and you some-times need to look carefully to see if something is listed as sponsored by a particular company, organization, or industry. Sponsored content can get tricky since it can be a form of bias. For instance, a company that sells blenders might sponsor an article about making smoothies and eating healthily. But this company probably wants to sell blenders, so they might say things in the article that subtly encourage you to buy one of their blenders.

A student told us

'Sometimes you get assignments that just tell you to use sources, but that can be really vague.'

That is very true. Knowing more about the different types of sources that exist can help you pick the right ones for your project. And, as you gain experience as a researcher, you'll start learning more about what types of sources are most appropriate for different types of projects.

'If you know what options exist, you can make informed and empowered decisions and choices.'

CHECK POINT — Reviewing your sources

What are some of the different types of sources that you have used in research projects in the past? Make a list here:

....

....

....

....

....

....

Now, review your list. Do you notice any trends in the types of sources you have used for certain types of projects? Write down your observations here!

....

....

....

....

....

....

How can I learn more about who created my source?

10 second
summary

Investigating the author and the publisher of a source, including their background, expertise, and reputation, can be an eye-opening experience and is crucial for determining the credibility of a source.

Probably the most important piece of investigation you can do with a source is to check on the author and publisher. Who is responsible for creating this source and making it available? The credibility, reputation, and expertise of an author or publisher has a direct impact on how credible your source is. After all, if an author does not have a background in, or expertise in, the topic of the article, then they probably are not going to be able to write a very informative article. Taking a moment to check on the author or the publisher of a source is one of the most efficient and effective ways to learn more about your source and get a sense of your source's credibility.

When you research the author or the publisher (meaning the magazine, journal, newspaper, or site where the source appears), you can learn a lot about their reputation, their past work, and their expertise. You can learn if they lack expertise or have a history of producing non-credible content. And the good news is that you can learn a huge amount with a basic Internet search! A quick search can often give a lot of information about an author or a publisher and, importantly, their reputation.

Here are a few things you can keep an eye out for when you are research-ing an author or a publisher and determining whether or not your source, and they, are credible:

- What sort of credentials and background does the author have? Do they seem like they have expertise on the topic and know what they are talking about?

- What sort of things has the author written in the past?

- What type of content does the publisher publish? Does the publisher have other content on your topic?

- What are others saying about your author and publisher? Do they seem to have good reputations?

Do I have to check out both the author and the publisher?

Answer: yes!

It is important to check up on both an author and a publisher when you are evaluating a source. You might have an author who is not credible but has published an article in an otherwise credible publication, or vice versa.

- **Example 1:** You might come across an op-ed in a respected newspaper. The op-ed is written by someone who holds controversial views on climate change, which are not supported by many experts. While the newspaper is credible overall, this particular author and article might raise some concerns and lack credibility on the topic.

- **Example 2:** You might come across a highly-credible article on a political issue in an unexpected source, such as a lifestyle magazine that normally publishes on more frivolous topics. While the magazine itself might not have a lot of deep expertise in politics, the article in question might be well researched and highly credible.

The credibility and expertise of an author and a publication might often match up. Generally speaking, a website dedicated to misinformation and conspiracy theories is not going to post something credible from a highly respected researcher. But you can have situations where a credible source appears in an unexpected place, and vice versa.

Source type matters

Remember, different types of sources are produced in different ways. The expertise required to produce an academic journal article is not really what you need to successfully write a credible news article. For example, a business news journalist might have a strong background in business and finance, but they might lack an advanced degree. Likewise, the editorial review process at a magazine is different than the peer review process in an academic journal. When you are evaluating the expertise of an author or a publisher, make sure you understand where the source is coming from and what type of source you are trying to evaluate.

Academic journal A journal that publishes academic or scholarly articles and works. It often focuses on a particular subject or discipline.

Go outside the source

When you are investigating an author and a publication, it is important to go outside of the source and see what others are saying and what else you can find online. Why is it important to do this? Well, consider the following example. If you find a publication, such as a journal or a magazine, and visit the About page, you're probably going to see a lot of positive and glowing information. A publication is probably not going to say that 'we publish misinformation and rumours' on their About page! Likewise, an author probably won't declare that they are a conspiracy theorist on their official author profile page on a website. In order to find out more, you need to run some searches online and see what other people are saying to get a fuller picture of the reputation and credentials of an author or a publication.

Develop your own expertise

As you develop your own expertise in your subject or in a future career field, you will get better at evaluating sources more generally, and at investigating authors and publishers in particular. You are likely to start seeing names you recognize or have publications that are very familiar to you. When checking up on an author, certain credentials will start to pop out at you as well. As you start to develop your expertise in certain subjects, and get further into your studies or your career, pay attention to the types of sources you encounter and who is responsible for producing those sources.

A student told us

'If you know how to use a search engine, you're well on your way to researching authors and publishers. It's a lot like looking up a celebrity or whoever you're trying to learn more about online!'

Yes! Researching an author or a publisher can involve a quick search in your preferred search engine. You will just be looking for different things, such as an author's credentials, as opposed to a celebrity's starring roles.

'Remember, it never hurts to look at things with a critical eye. Be inquisitive and curious!'

CHECK POINT   Understanding scholarly sources

Scholarly articles have some unique features, but they also have things in common with other types of credible sources, including popular ones.

Look at the factors below and see if you can sort out the ones that are unique to scholarly articles and the ones that apply to all sorts of credible sources! Circle the answer you think is correct.

- The author has a PhD or an advanced credential
  All credible sources / credible scholarly sources

- The article has gone through peer review
  All credible sources / credible scholarly sources

- The author has written on this topic before
  All credible sources / credible scholarly sources

- The author has a history of producing quality and credible content
  All credible sources / credible scholarly sources

- The article is published in a reputable publication
  All credible sources / credible scholarly sources

- The article features extensive references, such as footnotes, a bibliography, or a works cited page
  All credible sources / credible scholarly sources

Credible scholarly articles are ones where...	Credible sources are ones where...
The author has a PhD or an advanced credential	The author has written on this topic before but having a PhD or an advanced credential isn't required
The article has gone through peer review	The author has a history of producing quality and credible content
The article features extensive references, such as footnotes, a bibliography, or a works cited page	The article is published in a reputable publication

Reflect on the following questions and start developing a list of trusted sources:

* Think about your studies or your field. Do you have any go-to authors or publications that you use for different projects?

....

....

* Now think about hobbies or interests you have. What are your go-to places for information on those topics?

....

....

* What has led you to trust or rely on certain authors or publications in your studies and in your personal interests and hobbies?

....

....

* Select some of the authors and publications from your list and run through the source evaluation questions (see p.37). Do your authors and publications seem legit and accurate?

....

....

You now have a starter list of some trusted, go-to places to find credible sources! Keep adding to this list as you get more involved in a certain subject, topic, or field of interest.

How can I fact-check a claim?

10 second summary

It can be all too easy to get fooled by an inaccurate claim. Use guiding questions and indicators to know when and how to run an effective fact-check.

Fact-checking might be *the* critical information literacy skill of the 21st century. This is a bold statement, but fact-checking skills are increasingly necessary given the challenges of misinformation. When consuming information online, it can be very easy to skim quickly and take things at face value. Fact-checking is a way to make sure you do not get fooled by bogus information. But you don't want to go too far the other way and not trust any information! Aim for healthy skepticism, as opposed to trusting everything or trusting nothing. You can use questions and criteria to know when to fact-check. A general rule of thumb is the less you know about a topic or issue, the more you should fact-check to ensure that you aren't falling prey to non-credible information.

It can be tricky to know when and how to effectively fact-check a source. Maybe you are short on time, or maybe the source or claim seems okay and you feel like it is safe enough to use the source. Fact-checking

Fact-checking A process of confirming whether or not the claims in a source are accurate and true.

doesn't have to be overly time consuming or complicated, and even a brief fact-check can make the difference between sharing and inadvertently spreading false information online or stopping the spread of a rumour. Or, in another scenario, a fact-check can be the difference between avoiding citing a non-credible source in a paper or using incorrect information and getting a bad grade. Here are a few situations when it can be particularly important to take some time to fact-check a source:

- **Contentious issues** – It's always a good idea to fact-check sources that are dealing with highly-contentious issues, or issues where people tend to disagree. Issues that attract a lot of debate can also attract misinformation and more questionable sources.

- **Unknown or questionable sources** – If you aren't familiar with a source's author or publisher, or if you have some questions or concerns about the author or publisher, it is a good idea to do some fact-checking.

- **Lack of references** – If the source you found does not include any citations or references it is a good idea to fact-check the claims in the source. This can also apply if the source includes links that seem suspicious or do not really provide any information or back-up the claims being made.

- **Lack of knowledge** – If you know very little about a topic, be sure to fact-check sources you come across. It is much easier to be fooled by non-credible sources if you do not know much about the topic than if you have expertise and are able to more easily identify issues or problems with the source.

Remember, fact-checking doesn't happen in a vacuum! Fact-checking is part of your broader source evaluation strategy and you can consider what you know about the source type, the author and publisher, and other source evaluation criteria in conjunction with a fact-check. For instance, if a source is coming from a known and trusted location, and you know about the topic already, you might not spend as much time fact-checking the claims than if the source is coming from an unknown publication and covers an unfamiliar topic.

How to fact-check

If you identify a source that requires some fact-checking, there are a few strategies and tips that you can use to help you run a successful fact-check:

- **Run a search and see what others are saying** – A quick Internet search can help you get a sense of what others are saying about your topic and whether or not they disagree with the source you found and the claims you are investigating.

- **Visit a fact-checking website** – There are a number of helpful websites that fact-check different topics and issues and provide a breakdown of whether or not a claim is true or false. Some notable fact-checking sites include Snopes and PolitiFact.

- **Visit trusted publications and authors** – If you have questions about a source, see if a publication or author that you trust has written about the topic. Do they agree or disagree with the source that you have found?

- **Check the source's sources** – If the source includes any citations, references, or links, check those to see what they say and where they go. Do the references look credible and do they support the claims of the source?

Complicating factors

Fact-checking information online can be complicated by a few different factors. Here are some strategies you can use to overcome these
challenges:

- **Filter bubbles** – A filter bubble is essentially an echo chamber.
  A social media site, for example, can create a filter bubble where
  you see the same type of content over and over. This can end up
  reinforcing your views since you might not be seeing information
  that contradicts or challenges the type of content you keep seeing
  online. A way to overcome filter bubbles is to run searches in different
  locations and try out different search terms. You can go to a different
  news site or use a different search engine to see what others are
  saying about your topic. You can also try out different keywords or
  search terms to find information on your topic and see if that exposes
  you to different kinds of information. Online filter bubbles can be
  tricky to overcome since you might not even recognize that you are
  in one and that you have a skewed view of a topic. Using your source
  evaluation skills and being very deliberate and intentional about fact-
  checking can help you deal with the challenges posed by filter bubbles.

- **Misinformation** – Likewise, misinformation is increasingly found
  online and can be difficult to spot. Misinformation can also spread
  incredibly quickly on social media. As with filter bubbles, being
  deliberate and intentional about evaluating and fact-checking your
  sources can help you not get fooled. Misinformation often relies on
  speed to spread, so taking a bit of time to actually evaluate a source
  can help you avoid inadvertently spreading misinformation online
  because you shared something without properly checking it.

- **Breaking news** – In situations that are developing and changing
  quickly, it is a very good idea to fact-check and reflect on the
  information you are seeing. Taking a pause and checking on your
  source can help you avoid sharing rumours or being taken in by
  non-credible information. In a breaking news situation, sources can
  quickly get debunked and information can change rapidly, so being
  alert and using your critical evaluation skills is crucial.

Fact-checking doesn't have to be incredibly time-consuming. But, sometimes, you need to take some extra time with a source. Or you might be stumped and need some help to figure out what is going on with a source. Here are some tips for dealing with challenges around fact-checking:

- **High-stakes situation** – Maybe you are working on an important research paper for a class, or you've been tasked with completing a major project at your job. If you are working on a major project, be sure to take some extra time to fact-check your sources. You don't want to accidentally use inaccurate information and end up harming your reputation as a researcher in a high-stakes situation.

- **Critical issues** – If you are writing, commenting, or sharing information on a divisive or critical issue, take some extra time to ensure that you are putting factual and credible information out into the world. Too many major issues and debates are beset by misinformation, so take some extra time to fact-check your sources to ensure you don't inadvertently contribute to the misinformation problems we have.

- **Fact-checking challenges** – Sometimes, you might be dealing with a tricky or complex topic and you can't quite figure out what is going on with your source or if the information you are seeing is credible. That is okay! If you are feeling overwhelmed or unsure, reach out to an expert. A teacher or professor, a librarian, or an expert in the field can often provide you with guidance and help, and get you on the right track with finding credible sources.

A student told us

'Fact-checking feels like something only experts can do, but it's definitely something anyone can learn and get better at with practice!'

Absolutely. Fact-checking is something that you can practise, whether you are evaluating sources for a research project or you're checking up on something you read online. The more you practise, the more confident you'll be as a fact-checker.

'Always be willing to ask questions and to seek out more information!'

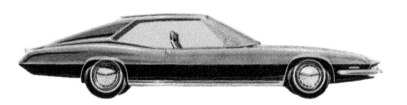

CHECK
POINT   Fact-checking sources

What are some of the situations where you may need to run a more extensive fact-check on a source? Write down a few examples here.

....

....

....

....

....

....

....

....

....

....

....

....

....

....

....

Speed fact-checking practice

Fact-checking can be particularly challenging online, since we often consume information quickly. This activity can help you practise your fact-checking skills and get more efficient:

1 Get on a social media site of your choice. Go through your feed and select an article or a post. Set a clock for 30 seconds and see if you can fact-check the information and determine if it is credible or not.

2 Repeat this and keep reducing the time you give yourself to fact-check claims. Go down to 20 seconds and then 10 seconds.

3 Reflect on how you did!

We often consume information incredibly quickly online and just skim headlines. What are some strategies that you can employ to help you better fact-check information that you come across online and in social media?

....

....

....

....

....

....

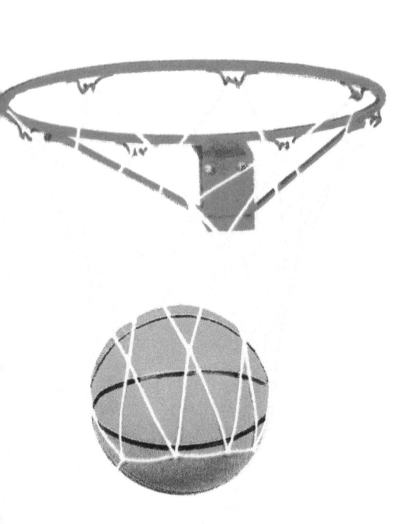

Congratulations!

You can now critically evaluate different types of sources, run fact-checks, and determine if a source is credible. You're now ready to use your knowledge to take a deeper dive into what your source is about and determine if a source is right for your research project or particular goal.

How can I identify the purpose of a source?

10 second
summary

Paying attention to factors like the
language and tone of a source can
help you gain important insight into the
overall purpose of a source and what
its goals are.

Use those literary analysis skills to analyse and determine the purpose of a source. Sources can have a wide range of purposes. They can inform, persuade, amuse, argue, or sadden. A source can try to make you feel something or think about something. It might want you to take some action or make a purchase. Sometimes a source can have a harmful purpose. For example, a source could be telling a lie or trying to scam you. Other times a source might have a purpose that isn't inherently good or bad but is certainly worth recognizing. You can use a lot of the skills you have picked up over the years in school to help you analyse and understand the purpose of a source, from paying attention to language choice to considering the tone.

Let's talk about bias

Bias is one of those things that can trip people up when they are trying to analyse a source. Is bias good or bad? And what even is it? Bias sometimes gets a bad rap, but it is essentially taking a side on an issue. Bias is not inherently good or bad, but it is important to recognize and understand bias when you see it in order to more fully understand and be able to evaluate your source. You wouldn't want to use a source as evidence in your research and share it as impartial when the source is, in fact, biased in a certain direction. It is important to remember that all humans have biases! We favour certain things or take certain stances or sides on different issues or have opinions. And biased humans can of course produce biased sources. A biased source can share an opinion or an argument that you might want to use in your own research, perhaps as an example of something you agree with or as a source you wish to argue against. The main thing here is that you recognize and acknowledge a source's bias when you use it or share it.

Types of purpose

Just as sources come in a variety of types, they also come with a variety of purposes. Here are a few common purposes that you might come across:

- **Inform** – Some sources are just trying to provide information and facts. News sources are often informative, in that they are reporting on events and not adding opinion or commentary. Likewise, something from an encyclopedia can fall into this category.

- **Persuade** – Other sources have opinions or bias or take a stance on an issue. Persuasive sources can come in a lot of different forms, whether it is someone's YouTube video where they are sharing an opinion on a controversy or an op-ed piece in a paper arguing for a certain type of political reform. You can use a persuasive source in your research and persuasive sources can be quite credible.

A persuasive source that is produced by an expert and features facts and accurate information to support its claims and arguments can be considered credible.

- **Sell** – Sources can also be trying to sell you something. A source that is trying to sell something can take the form of an advertisement or perhaps a product review or a list of best products to consider in a certain category.

- **Satirize** – Satire is where a source is using humour to comment on society or a particular social issue. Satire can be presented seriously but is in fact making fun of its subject or main topic.

- **Misinform** – Misinformation can take many forms, but sources that fall into this category are not credible and could be trying to fool someone or get someone to subscribe to inaccurate information.

Can sources have good purposes or bad purposes?

Some sources might have harmful purposes. A source might be trying to spread rumours or false information, or trying to fool or scam you, or trying to encourage you to act in a harmful manner. But other sources are not really good or bad, per se. For example, a source that is trying to sell something is not necessarily bad, but it is important to recognize the source for what it is and not assume that the source is an impartial information piece, as opposed to an advertisement. Remember, the key here is to recognize the purpose of a source and not think the source is saying or doing one thing when it is in fact doing something else entirely.

Identifying the purpose

When you are trying to identify the purpose of a source, you can draw upon a lot of skills that you are likely to have developed in school, such as in literature or writing courses.

- **Pay attention to the language and tone** – What is your source saying and how is it saying it? The language, style, and tone of a source can give you insight into what the source's purpose and goals are. Does the source seem informative and fairly dry? Is the source using impassioned language and making emotional appeals? Is the source making you laugh?

- **Look for a thesis or main points** – See if you can identify any main points or a main argument in your source. Does the author express a goal, or are they trying to make a certain argument?

- **Consider other credibility indicators** – Source evaluation considers a lot of factors and does not happen in a vacuum! Consider other aspects of your source, including the source type, the author, if the claims are factual, etc., to help you determine what is going on with the source and what the main goals are.

A student told us

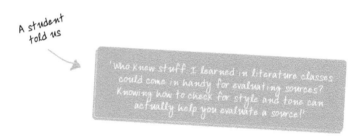

'Who knew stuff I learned in literature classes could come in handy for evaluating sources? Knowing how to check for style and tone can actually help you evaluate a source!'

You can use a lot of your past classes and experiences to help you evaluate sources. Even your daily Internet searches can help you develop your search skills and get better at performing evaluation tasks, like checking out an author's credentials.

'Sometimes an answer won't be immediately obvious. It is okay to take some time to reflect, explore, and examine different possibilities.'

Mapping the purpose

Sources can have a variety of purposes and identifying the purpose of a source can involve looking at a lot of factors. To help make sense of this, select a source and try creating a mind map to keep track of your observations. Jot down words that describe the tone, draw connections between interesting factors, etc. See what your visual map can reveal to you!

How do I know if a source is worth using?

10 second
summary

Every research project is different and
has unique needs, so it's important
to evaluate your source to determine
whether or not it is the right one for your
research project.

Sources can make or break your research project. If you select sources that aren't appropriate for your project, your research might come across as unfocused, confusing, or even not credible. It is important to not just evaluate your sources for credibility but to also evaluate your sources for whether or not they are the right fit for your particular research project and your research needs. Reflecting on what your project is about, what your goals are, what your research questions are, and what you need for your research project to be successful, whether it's a large-scale project or something relatively small, can help you make sure that you are finding the best sources for your project.

Not all sources will work for your research projects and information needs. Aside from evaluating sources for credibility, you also need to determine what your goals and needs are and decide if a particular source is right for you. You might need to find scholarly information for a research paper that you need to complete for a class, or you might be looking for something short and sweet to share online. Maybe you just want to learn more about a topic, or maybe you need in-depth information to help you make an important financial decision. And sometimes the best source might be something that is not all that credible! For instance, you might want to use a source that takes a faulty stance on an issue in order to demonstrate a point or provide a counterargument. Part of evaluating sources is understanding what you are seeing and how you can use that source in your particular project.

Projects might call for different kinds of sources

Here are a few examples of how your information needs can differ, depending on your project:

Example 1 – you actually need misinformation.

You might actually be trying to highlight the misinformation that is impacting the debate on a hot-button issue. In this situation, you might deliberately try to find and use misinformation in your project. The information isn't credible but your project's goals and needs mean that it is appropriate to include non-credible information, in this case. The key thing here is that you are acknowledging what the misinformation is and not trying to pass it off as credible.

Example 2 – you are deliberately using sources you don't agree with to argue your point.

Sometimes, particularly if you are engaging in a debate, you might want to seek out information you don't agree with in order to provide a counterargument in your paper. You can use sources that say the opposite of what you think to set up an argument, engage in a debate in your paper, and explain to a reader why you disagree with the source and what you think instead.

> **Counterargument** An argument that opposes an idea or view proposed in another argument.

Example 3 – you are writing a term paper needing scholarly sources.

Sometimes you might be instructed to use a certain kind of source. For instance, if you are writing a research paper for school your instructor might tell you to use scholarly sources. In this case, even if you found a great magazine article, you wouldn't want to use it in your paper.

The power of the annotated bibliography

You may have written an annotated bibliography for a past project. Annotated bibliographies are a really incredible framework for helping you evaluate sources and decide if they are right for your project. In a typical annotated bibliography, you provide a brief summary of a source and then evaluate whether or not you will be using the source in your project. You can explain your reasoning for using, or not using, a given source. You can actually use this framework in a scaled down way to help you evaluate sources for any project. Remember, you don't want to just evaluate a source for credibility. You also want to determine if it is right for you.

A student told us

'I was always just focused on finding any source and not really considering whether it was the best source for me. Having a research plan and knowing how to evaluate sources makes it way easier to find the best sources for a project.'

This is very true. Taking some time to develop a research plan and to evaluate your sources can help you have success with your research projects and be a confident and savvy researcher.

'Don't be afraid to ask questions, and don't be afraid to ask for help! Sometimes we need some extra support to find the answers and information we need.'

CHECK POINT Determining value

Remember, you can determine if a source is right for you by answering the following questions:

- What is this source saying?

- How might I use this source in my research?

- Does this source seem appropriate for my research needs?

- What other kinds of sources might I need? Am I missing anything?

- Does this source reference other works that I might want to explore?

| ACTIVITY | Evaluate sources with an annotated bibliography |

For each source, write down and answer the following to help you evaluate your source and decide if it is right for your needs:

Source information, including title and author:

....

Where did you find this source?

....

What search terms did you use to find your source?

....

Provide a summary of your source:

....

....

....

....

....

Use the evaluation criteria (see p.32) and explain whether or not this source is credible. Remember to pay particular attention to the author and publisher, the accuracy of the claims, and the purpose of the source.

....

....

....

....

How do you think you could use this source in your research project or for your research need?

....

....

....

....

What is your final verdict – is this source appropriate for your project or not?

....

....

....

....

Final checklist: How to know you are done

Have you:

Identified your research needs and goals? ☐

Identified the types of sources you need for your research? ☐

Found a source? ☐

Identified the type of source you found? ☐

Used the credibility indicators to determine if the source
is credible? ☐

Explored the author and publisher to determine if they have
expertise in the topic? ☐

Fact-checked the source to ensure the claims are accurate? ☐

Determined the purpose of the source? ☐

Decided whether or not the source is right for your
research needs? ☐

Glossary

Academic journal A journal that publishes academic or scholarly articles and works. It often focuses on a particular subject or discipline.

Bias Strong weight in favour of, or against, a certain idea or topic.

Conspiracy theory A belief in some sort of idea or explanation that is false and is not based in fact or reality.

Counterargument An argument that opposes an idea or view proposed in another argument.

Credibility Something that is trusted and believed in. Credible sources have factors, such as accuracy and expertise, that help people view them as trustworthy.

Digital citizen Someone using digital tools and information technology to engage in society and in different social and political issues.

Evaluate To assess or analyse something. In the context of evaluating sources, evaluation means determining whether or not a source is credible.

Fact-checking A process of confirming whether or not the claims in a source are accurate and true.

Factual Something that is true and focuses on reality and what is actually the case, rather than interpretation.

Information literacy A skill set that involves the ability to find, use, evaluate, produce, and share information in a variety of formats.

Misinformation False or inaccurate information that may deliberately try to deceive someone.

Opinion A belief or a view that may or may not be based on fact.

Peer review A review process where experts in a field review the work of another expert to ensure that it is accurate and worthy of publication.

Popular source   A wide range of sources that are not scholarly. Popular sources vary greatly in terms of type and credibility.

Primary source   A source of information created at a time of study. Primary sources can take many forms, such as diaries, letters, or newsreel footage, and may provide a first-hand account of a past event or a topic.

Scholarly source   An academic source that is written by experts and is subject to peer review.

Source   Material that you can use to provide evidence in a research project or to fulfil an information need. Sources can come in many forms and can be used for a variety of purposes.

Trade publication   A publication that focuses on providing news, updates, and information for a specific industry.

Next steps

Visit or email your local library! Librarians are always happy to help you find and evaluate sources.

Check out resources for fact-checkers! There are some great websites out there to help you learn more about fact-checking and source evaluation:

Snopes – www.snopes.com

NewsGuard – www.newsguardtech.com

Poynter MediaWise resources – www.poynter.org/mediawise

FactCheck.org at the Annenberg Center – www.factcheck.org

Milton Keynes UK
Ingram Content Group UK Ltd.
UKHW021500251124
3115UKWH00032B/340